SECOND GRADE SCIENCE
SEMESTER A

ACCELERATE EDUCATION

Table of Contents

Module 1 1

Module 2 9

Module 3 15

Module 4 21

Module 5 29

Module 6 39

Module 7 47

Module 8 55

Module 9 60

Module 10 66

Module 11 67

Module 12 71

Module 13 80

Module 14 87

Module 15 93

Module 16 99

Module 17 101

Module 18 107

Cutout Worksheets 112

This workbook contains all of the worksheets found in the Science 2 Semester A course. To see the worksheet in color, view it online within the lessons. For any worksheets containing cutting activities, they can be found in the "Cutout Worksheets" section.

© 2023 by Accelerate Education
Visit us on the Web at www.accelerate.education

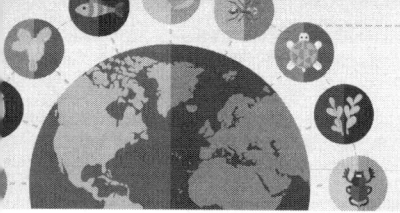 

SCIENCE

Name: _____ Date: _____

Senses Sleuth

Directions: Use your five senses to complete the following activities.

Seeing Activity:

1. Look at each picture below. Then decide if the items are the same or different.

   a. Circle: Same   or   Different?

   b. How do you know?
   _____
   _____
   _____

   c. Circle: Same   or   Different?

   d. How do you know?
   _____
   _____
   _____

Next Page

1

1.1 The Five Senses

Hearing Activity:

2. Find a room nearby and describe the sounds.

   Room you picked:_____

What Do You Hear?	What is Making the Sound?

Smelling Activity:

3. Find three items that have a specific smell. Give each item a sniff and record if it smelled good, bad, or neither.

Item	Description of Smell

Next Page

1.1 The Five Senses

Touching Activity:

4. Find four items and place them in a bag. Close your eyes and put your hand in the bag. Feel each item, and try to guess what it is. Record your observations below.

Item	Description

Tasting Activity:

5. Find the three foods pictured below on the plates. Taste them and then under each plate, describe the taste. Is it sweet? Salty? Sour? Bland?

It tastes...

It tastes...

It tastes...

3

1.1 The Five Senses

SCIENCE

Name: _____ Date: _____

Sleep & Heart Rate Study

Part I: Sleep Study

Directions: Each night this week write down the time you went to bed. In the morning, write down the time you wake up. Then, figure out how many hours you slept. Also, mark how you feel when you wake up.

	Time you went to bed	Time you woke in morning	Total sleep time	In the morning, how did you feel?
Date: _____	_____P.M.	_____A.M.	_____Hour _____Minutes	☐ Tired ☐ Refreshed
Date: _____	_____P.M.	_____A.M.	_____Hour _____Minutes	☐ Tired ☐ Refreshed
Date: _____	_____P.M.	_____A.M.	_____Hour _____Minutes	☐ Tired ☐ Refreshed
Date: _____	_____P.M.	_____A.M.	_____Hour _____Minutes	☐ Tired ☐ Refreshed
Date: _____	_____P.M.	_____A.M.	_____Hour _____Minutes	☐ Tired ☐ Refreshed

Next Page

1.2 Human Patterns

1. Did you get about nine and a half hours of sleep each night?

2. What can you predict might happen to you if you do not get enough sleep for a few days?

Part 2: Heart Rate Study

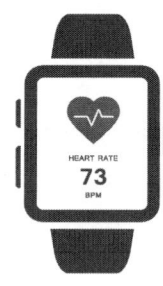

Directions: Do some heartbeat trials just as Jake and Bianca did. Follow the directions to find your resting heart rate and your heart rate after exercise.

Find your heart rate:

- Turn one hand so your palm is facing upward.
- Place the first two fingers of your other hand next to the bone on the edge of your wrist (on the thumb side of your wrist).
- Move your fingers slowly around until you find your pulse.

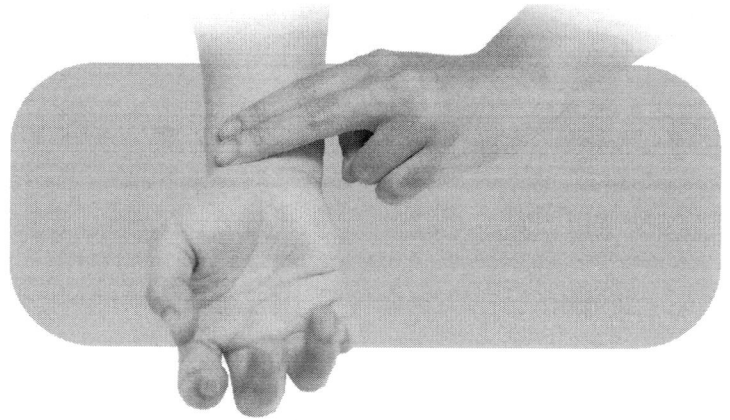

- Watch a clock with a second hand, or a smartwatch or timer.
- Count the number of beats in 15 seconds.
- Multiply this number by 4 to find your beats per minute.

3. Sit down for at least 2-3 minutes. Then, measure your heart rate. This will be your resting heart rate. Then, do ten jumping jacks and measure your heart rate again. Finally, jog in place for one minute. Measure your heart rate again. Repeat this process three times. Make sure you rest in between.

	Trial 1	Trial 2	Trial 3
Resting heart rate			
After doing ten jumping jacks			
After jogging in place for one minute			

4. What did you notice about your heart rate after you did some exercise?

5. Why is it important for your heart rate to go up when you exercise?

1.2 Human Patterns

SCIENCE

Name: _____ Date: _____

Animal Communication

Part 1: Communicating with Pets

Directions: Answer the following questions.

1. How do you communicate with your parents or friends?
   _____
   _____
   _____
   _____

2. How do you communicate with an animal or pet?
   _____
   _____
   _____
   _____

3. How is communicating with a pet different from communicating with a friend?
   _____
   _____
   _____
   _____

Next Page

1.3 Communicating With Pets

Part 2: Collecting Information about Pets

Directions: Look at each picture to predict what the pet is feeling. Read each heading. In each box, describe the body part listed in one or two words. Then decide what you think the pet is feeling. The first row has been completed for you as an example.

	Eyes	Ears	Mouth	Body	What might the pet be feeling?
	relaxed	relaxed	closed	on back	calm / happy

1.3 Communicating With Pets

8

SCIENCE

Name: _____ Date: _____

Basic Needs of Animals

Directions: Think about the basic needs of all animals. Draw an animal's environment and explain how that animal meets its basic needs.

1. Draw a picture of any animal that was not discussed in the lesson. In your drawing, include the animal's environment.

Next Page

2.1 Animal Needs

2. Explain the needs of the animal you drew and how the animal's needs are met.

_____
_____
_____
_____
_____
_____
_____
_____

3. Circle the category your animal falls into.

CARNIVORE   HERBIVORE

OMNIVORE   INSECTIVORE

2.1 Animal Needs

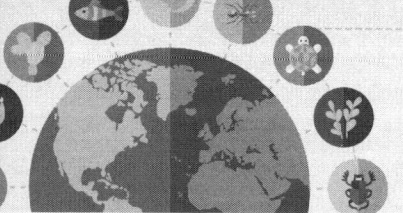 

SCIENCE

Name: _____ Date: _____

Where Does Your Animal Live?

Directions: Choose an animal that lives in your area and complete the following activities.

1. Create a model of your chosen animal's home or where it lives. You can either take a picture of your model and paste it in the box or draw a picture of your model below.

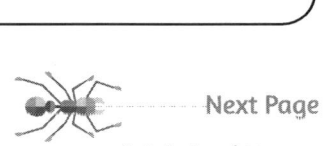

Next Page

11 | 2.2 Animal Homes

2. What does your animal use for shelter? Why does it use this for shelter?

_____
_____
_____
_____
_____
_____
_____
_____
_____
_____
_____
_____
_____
_____
_____
_____

SCIENCE

Name: _____ Date: _____

Your Investigation

Directions: Choose one question from the list below. Then answer the questions that follow.

- Why do tigers have stripes?
- What does a squirrel need to be healthy?
- What is a companion animal?
- Are all birds' nests the same?

1. What question did you select?

   _____
   _____
   _____
   _____

2. What observations and research do you need to do?

   _____
   _____
   _____
   _____

3. What is your hypothesis?

   _____
   _____
   _____
   _____

Next Page

13   2.3 Investigating Animal Needs

Now go to the library with your learning coach. Find a book that will help you gather information and answer your question. You may also ask the librarian or your learning coach to help you do an Internet search.

4. What is the answer to your question?

_____
_____
_____
_____
_____
_____
_____
_____

SCIENCE

Name: _____ Date: _____

Animal Senses

Directions: Label each column with one of the five senses. Draw a picture of an animal in each column showing how the animal uses that sense. Then write 1-2 sentences explaining how the animal is using that specific sense.

15

Next Page

3.2 Animal Senses

3.2 Animal Senses

SCIENCE

Name: _____ Date: _____

Drawing Conclusions about Animals

Directions: Study the chart below. Fill in the missing parts based on the reasons, examples, senses, or pictures given.

Reason	Example	Sense	Picture
to claim territory	a tiger spraying its scent		
	a dog barking	hearing	
to find members of its group	a bird or wolf calling		
to show affection		touch	

Next Page

17

3.3 The Five Senses and Animal Communication

Reason	Example	Sense	Picture
to find a mate	male birds having bright feathers		
	a lion showing its teeth	sight	
to show acceptance	monkeys grooming each other		
	baby deer sniffing adults' legs	smell	

3.3 The Five Senses and Animal Communication

SCIENCE

Name: _____ Date: _____

Guess the Animal

Directions:

1. Choose a wild animal. Conduct your investigation by doing research either through an Internet search or in a book at the library about your wild animal.
2. In Box 1, draw a picture of your animal and write the animal's name.
3. In Box 2, draw a picture of the tracks your animal makes. Label your animal as a bounder, galloper, pacer, or diagonal walker.
4. In Box 3, describe ways that your animal uses its five senses to meet its needs in its environment.
5. In Box 4, describe how your animal communicates to meet its needs.
6. In Box 5, write about where your animal is located and the type of shelter, they live in.
7. In Box 6, describe the type of food your animal needs to eat to survive.
8. Cover up your animal in Box 1 with a sticky note. Ask your learning coach or another adult to guess what your animal is after he or she reads your description!

Next Page

19　　3.4 Project: Guess the Animal

Box 1: My animal is...	Box 2: Animal Tracks

Box 3: Five Senses	Box 4: Communication

Box 5: Location/Shelter	Box 6: Food Source

3.4 Project: Guess the Animal

SCIENCE

Name: _____   Date: _____

Paper Airplane Challenge

Directions: Can you build a paper airplane that will fly in the air? Use the flow chart to work through the engineering design process. Then complete the trial chart and answer the questions.

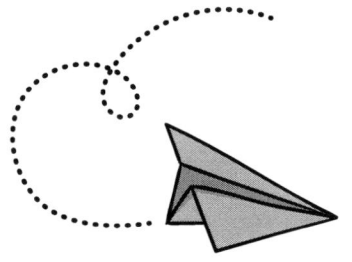

1. Use the design process to build your paper airplane.

a. Ask: What is the problem?

b. Imagine: What are the solutions?

c. Plan: Draw your design. Gather your materials.

d. Create: Build a prototype. Describe or take a picture and paste here.

e. Improve: Test and make improvements. Describe your tests and improvements.

Next Page

21   4.1 Solving Problems

2. Now test and improve your airplane. Chart your data.

	Did it fly?	Distance flown in inches	Improvements made
Trial 1			
Trial 2			
Trial 3			

3. What went well in your design process?

_____
_____
_____

4. What are two things you learned in this process?

_____
_____
_____

5. Describe your final design.

_____
_____
_____

4.1 Solving Problems

SCIENCE

Name: _____   Date: _____

Wear a Solution

Directions: Think of a problem that you can solve by designing something you can wear using materials you have around your house or neighborhood. Then start to define your problem by working through the ask and imagine steps of the engineering design process. Answer the questions about your problem.

1. What is a problem you can try to solve?
   _____
   _____
   _____

2. What requirements will your idea need (cost, time, materials)?
   _____
   _____
   _____

3. What limits will you have when creating your idea?
   _____
   _____
   _____

Next Page

4.2 Defining a Problem

Directions: Brainstorm a list of as many solutions as possible. Remember the limits and requirements you wrote above. Then choose the best solution you think you can work with.

4. Brainstorm:

_____
_____
_____
_____
_____
_____
_____
_____
_____
_____

5. What is your best solution?

_____
_____
_____

4.2 Defining a Problem

SCIENCE

Name: _____ Date: _____

Create Your Wearable Solution!

Directions: Continue to work through the engineering design process by completing the final steps to create your product. You may use actual materials and work through the steps, or just write how you think things would go if you had the materials to build your product. Answer the questions about your problem.

1. What was the best idea for your wearable solution?
   _____
   _____
   _____
   _____

2. Sketch your idea in the box below. Be sure to label your sketch with materials and parts.

   [sketch box]

   Next Page

25   4.3 Testing a Solution

Directions: Build your prototype. Then answer the questions about your prototype.

3. What does your prototype look like?

   _____
   _____
   _____
   _____

4. What struggles and accomplishments did you have while building your prototype?

   _____
   _____
   _____
   _____

Directions: Test your prototype. Then answer the questions about the prototype testing.

5. How did you test your prototype?

   _____
   _____
   _____
   _____

Next Page

4.3 Testing a Solution

26

6. What problems did you have with your prototype?

_____
_____
_____
_____

7. What are your ideas to solve those problems?

_____
_____
_____
_____

Directions: Use the ideas that you just generated to improve your prototype. Then answer the questions about the process.

8. What improvements did you make?

_____
_____
_____
_____
_____
_____

Next Page

4.3 Testing a Solution

Directions: Test your prototype again. Then answer the questions about the prototype testing.

9. Did the improvements work?
_____
_____
_____

10. How many times did you have to test and improve your product to get a working product?
_____
_____
_____
_____

11. Describe your final product.
_____
_____
_____
_____
_____

4.3 Testing a Solution

SCIENCE

Name: _____ Date: _____

Matter: Observe and Predict

Directions: Gather six objects from around your house or yard. Make sure the items are safe to put in water! List the items in the chart below and draw a picture of each.

Use at least three properties to describe each object (size, shape, color, texture, or flexibility). Next, make a prediction. Do you think the item will sink or float?

Fill a tub, sink, or other container with water. Put each item in the water. Be sure to record the results! The first row has been completed for you as an example.

Name and Picture	Description	Sink or Float Prediction	Sink or Float Results
 Metal Spoon	shiny, silver, small, hard, smooth	float	sink

Next Page

29

5.1 Introduction to Matter

Name and Picture	Description	Sink or Float Prediction	Sink or Float Results

5.1 Introduction to Matter

SCIENCE

Name: _____   Date: _____

Questions about Matter

Directions: Follow the steps below to answer questions about the teddy bear in the picture.

1. Observe the teddy bear in the photo.

2. Create four more questions you can ask about an object to identify its properties. Ask questions about all the properties (texture, shape, size, and color). Write one question at the top of each empty column in the chart.

   - For example, you might ask, "Is it soft?" The answer could then lead you to identify that one property of the teddy bear is that it is soft. That example has already been added to the chart.

3. Ask each question in your chart about the teddy bear. Add your answers to the second row.

Next Page

31

5.2 Properties of Matter

4. Choose nine more objects from around your home. List the objects in the nine empty rows in the chart.

5. Analyze each object by asking and answering your questions in the top row. When you are done, every box in the chart should have something written in it.

Object	It is soft?				
teddy bear	yes				

5.2 Properties of Matter

SCIENCE

Name: _____ Date: _____

Create a Bridge

Directions: It is time to create your own bridge! Using two stacks of books, create your own bridge that will span from one end of the books to the other. Your bridge should be sturdy enough for a toy car to travel from one end to the other.

Materials:
- 3" x 5" index cards
- 6 books
- tape
- string
- toy car

Purpose:
- Build a bridge that will span across two stacks of books that are about six inches apart. Challenge yourself by making your bridge span wider than six inches!

Next Page

33 5.3 Engineering Properties of Matter

Ask

1. What is the purpose of your design?

Imagine

2. Imagine how you can build a bridge using the materials you have been given. Draw a quick design of the parts you think you will need to include. Answer these questions and any others you can think of:

   a. Does your bridge have to be long or short?
   b. How tall should your bridge be?
   c. How strong does your bridge need to be?

Next Page

5.3 Engineering Properties of Matter

Plan

3. What will your bridge look like? Sketch a design in the space below.

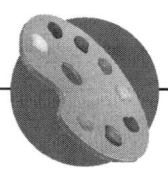

Create

4. Build your bridge according to your sketch using the materials you listed. Take a picture of your bridge and paste it below.

Next Page

5.3 Engineering Properties of Matter

Test 1

5. It is time to test your design! Place the car on the bridge and see what happens. Write a brief summary of your first attempt. What went well? Write your notes under **Positive** below. What needs to improve? Write your notes under **Things to improve** below.

1st attempt:

a. Positive:
_____
_____
_____

b. Things to improve:
_____
_____
_____

Improve

6. Reflect on what went well and what you think you can improve. Answer the question below.

a. **What changes can you make to improve your bridge?**
_____
_____
_____
_____

Make these changes to your bridge.

Test 2

7. It is time to test your improved design! Place the car on the bridge and see what happens. Write a brief summary of your second attempt. What went well? What needs to improve?

2nd attempt:

a. Positive:
_____
_____
_____
_____

b. Things to improve:
_____
_____
_____
_____

Improve

8. Reflect on what went well and what you think you can improve. Answer the questions below.

a. What changes can you make to improve your bridge?
_____
_____
_____
_____

b. Make the changes and try again! How did the third attempt go after reflecting and making changes?
_____
_____
_____
_____

Next Page

5.3 Engineering Properties of Matter

Take a picture of your final design and paste it here!

SCIENCE

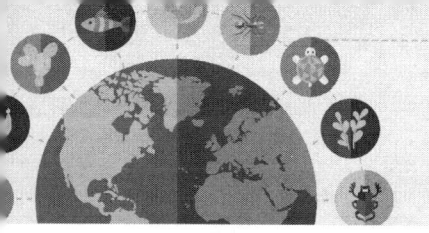

Name: _____ Date: _____

Matter Scavenger Hunt

Directions: Look for three examples of each state of matter. Write the word or draw a picture of the example in the correct column.

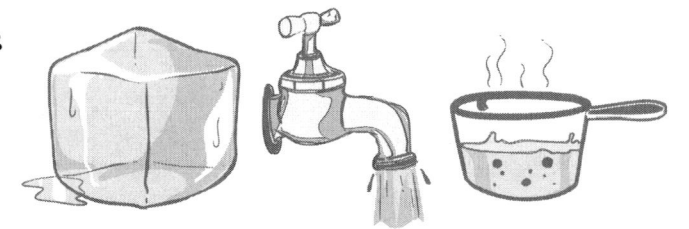

Solid	Liquid	Gas

Next Page

39

6.1 States of Matter

Answer the following questions about states of matter.

1. What state of matter did you observe most often?

2. What state of matter did you observe least often?

3. If you stick your finger into water and pull it back out, the water fills back in where your finger was. Why?

4. You can easily walk through gases that make up our air. Why?

6.1 States of Matter

SCIENCE

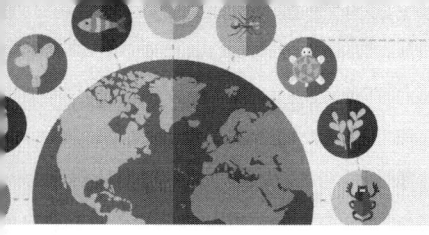

Name: _____ Date: _____

Changes in Water

Directions: Investigate how cooling and heating change the state of water. You will need the materials listed below.

Materials:
- water
- ice cube tray or small container

Follow these steps:

1. Put water in an ice cube tray or small container.
2. Put the ice cube tray or container in the freezer.
3. Wait 4 - 5 hours until it is solid.
4. Pull out the tray or container after the water becomes frozen.
5. Put a small ice cube or block in your hand.
6. Observe what happens to the ice in your hand.

Next Page

41

6.2 Changes in Matter

Answer the following questions.

1. What changes of states did you see?

2. What caused the ice to change from a solid to a liquid?

3. What caused the water to change from a liquid to a solid?

4. What could you do to change the water from a liquid to a gas?

6.2 Changes in Matter

SCIENCE

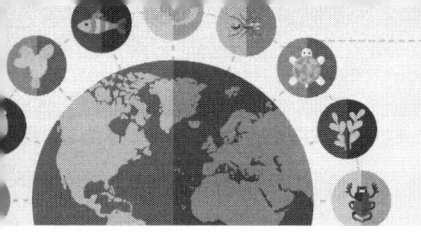

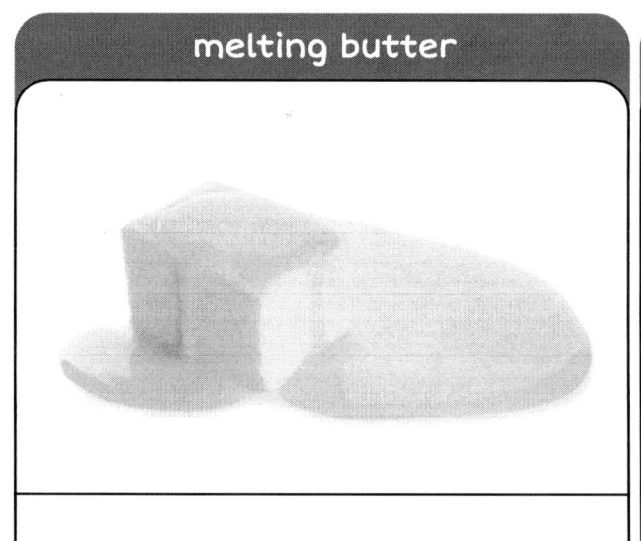

Name: _____ Date: _____

Reversible vs. Irreversible Changes

Directions: Look at each picture below. Decide if the change is reversible or irreversible. Under each picture, write the word reversible or irreversible.

Reversible change:
- when something can be returned to its original state

Irreversible change:
- when something cannot be returned to its original state

melting butter	toasting bread

Next Page

43

6.3 Investigating Matter

breaking a vase	boiling water
rusting nails	bending a paper clip

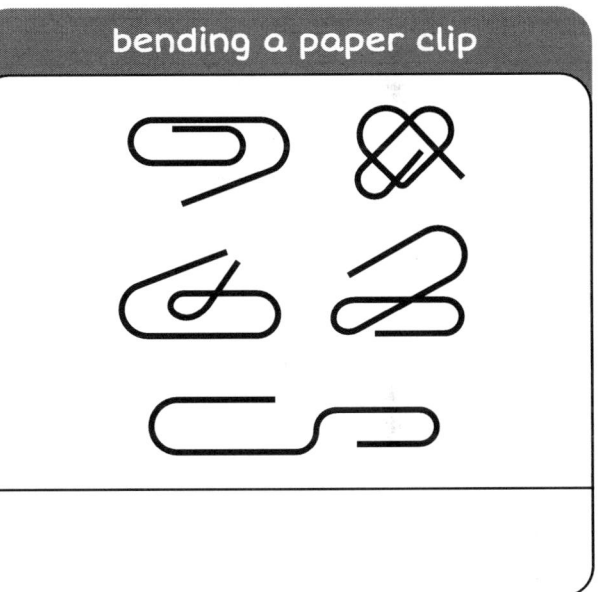

6.3 Investigating Matter

44

SCIENCE

Name: _____ Date: _____

Changing Matter

Directions: As you complete the instructions for your chosen activity, please fill in the boxes below. Fill in an answer as directed in the lesson.

1. **Circle** the name of the investigation you chose: Cloud in a Jar | Mystery Matter

Box 1

2. Make a hypothesis about what you think will happen.

Box 2

3. Explain how this experiment is an example of matter.

Next Page

45

6.4 Project: Changing Matter

Box 3

4. Can the matter in this experiment be reversed? Why or why not?

6.4 Project: Changing Matter

SCIENCE

Name: _____ Date: _____

Tracking Temperatures

Directions: Using an outdoor thermometer or a weather app on your device, record the temperature outside for five days. Then answer the questions about heat and temperature.

1. On the chart below, record the outside temperature for the next five days in degrees Fahrenheit.

	Day 1	Day 2	Day 3	Day 4	Day 5
Temperature					

2. Based on the data you recorded, were any of the days hot? How do you know?

_____
_____
_____
_____
_____

Next Page

7.1 Heat and Temperature

3. Look at the objects in each row below. Draw an arrow in the middle column showing the direction in which the heat is moving between the two objects.

7.1 Heat and Temperature

2. What do you observe about your structure?

_____
_____
_____
_____
_____

3. With your learning coach, find two solid ingredients, like fruits and vegetables, in the kitchen to combine. Then complete the chart below.

	Observations of the substances before combining	Observations after combining the substances
substance 1		
substance 2		

4. With your learning coach, find water and salt or sugar in the kitchen to combine. Then complete the chart below.

	Observations of the substances before combining	Observations after combining the substances
salt / sugar		
water		

7.2 Combining Substances

SCIENCE

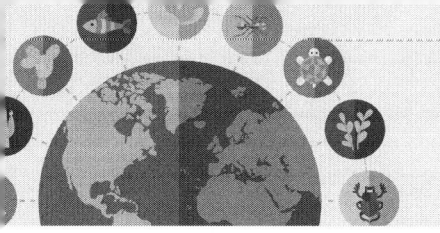

Name: _____ Date: _____

Keep Your Cup Cozy

Directions: Investigate to see what materials can keep a cup of hot water warm the longest.

Step 1: Gather the following materials:

- 4 plastic cups
- materials for wrapping the cups, such as bubble wrap, aluminum foil, plastic bags, newspaper, cardboard, or fabric
- tape or rubber bands
- a large, shallow baking pan
- one or two trays of ice cubes
- hot and cold tap water
- thermometer
- timer

Step 2: Create a hypothesis for your investigation.

- What materials do you think will keep the cup of water warm for the longest time?

_____
_____
_____
_____
_____

Next Page

7.3 Insulation   52

Step 3: Complete your investigation by following these steps:

a. Choose three materials to test. Wrap each material around one plastic cup. Use tape or rubber bands to hold the material on each cup.* Make sure that each cup still stands up straight after it is wrapped. Leave one cup unwrapped. In the chart on the next page, record what materials you chose for insulation.

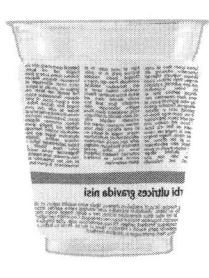

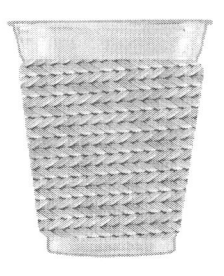

*If your material is not waterproof, you might want to put a plastic bag around it. If you need to put one of the cups in a plastic bag, put all of them in a plastic bag to keep them the same.

b. Put the ice cubes in the baking pan. Add enough cold water to fill the pan about 1 to 2 inches deep. Wait about 10 minutes for the water to get ice cold. If all the ice cubes melt, add some more.

c. Have your learning coach help you pour hot tap water into the four plastic cups. Fill each one about 2 inches deep. Use a thermometer to measure the temperature of the water in each cup. Record the temperatures in the chart.

d. Place all four cups in the pan of ice water.

e. Wait 10 minutes, and then measure the temperature of the water in the cups again. When you move the thermometer from one cup to another, remember to wait until the level of the thermometer liquid stops moving before you record the temperature. Record the temperatures in the chart.

f. Do #5 two more times, so that you have recorded the temperature after 10, 20, and 30 minutes.

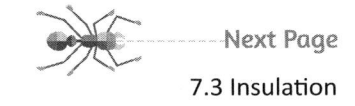

Next Page

7.3 Insulation

Step 4: Record your observations in the chart.

Insulation Observation Chart

	Cup 1	Cup 2	Cup 3	Cup 4
Insulation Material				None
Temperature at start				
Temperature after 10 min.				
Temperature after 20 min.				
Temperature after 30 min.				

Step 5: Answer the following questions:

a. Which cup cooled off the fastest?

b. Which cup cooled off most slowly?

c. Which material was the best insulation? How can you tell?

7.3 Insulation

SCIENCE

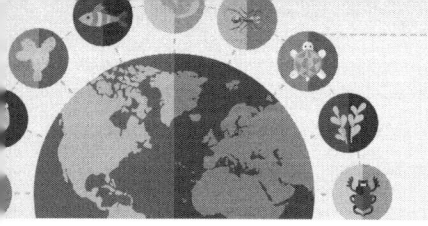

Name: _____ Date: _____

Animal Habitats

Directions: Describe each habitat in a few words. Then draw and label a picture of an animal that can live in that habitat.

Habitat	Description	Animal
Ocean		
Arctic		
Rainforest		
Desert		
Grasslands		
Wetlands		

Next Page

55

8.1 Animal Habitats

1. Choose one animal that you learned about in this lesson. Draw a picture of the animal in its habitat.

Name of animal:

2. Explain how this specific animal can survive in its habitat.

_____
_____
_____
_____

8.1 Animal Habitats

SCIENCE

Name: _____ Date: _____

Animal Changes in Winter

Directions: Choose an animal that falls under each category. Draw a picture of your animal. Then answer each question.

1. Hibernation is a deep sleep that helps animals save energy and survive the winter without eating much.

My animal is a _____

a. Draw a picture of your animal.

b. Provide three facts explaining how your animal hibernates.
_____
_____
_____
_____
_____
_____

c. Why does this animal hibernate?
_____
_____
_____
_____
_____

Next Page

57 8.2 Animals and Seasons

2. Migration means that animals move to places with warmer weather where plenty of food is available.

My animal is a _____

a. Draw a picture of your animal.

b. Provide three facts explaining how your animal migrates.

c. Why does this animal migrate?

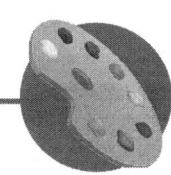

8.2 Animals and Seasons

58

SCIENCE

Name: _____ Date: _____

Design Your Own Squirrel Habitat

Directions: Think about a time when you saw a squirrel. Use your personal experience and the information that you learned in this lesson to create a squirrel habitat.

1. Draw and color a squirrel's habitat, and label the items that you put in your drawing. Give your squirrel a name, and write in the bubble something you think your squirrel would say if it could talk.

2. Write two sentences explaining your squirrel's habitat.
_____
_____
_____

8.3 Squirrel Habitats

SCIENCE

Name: _____ Date: _____

Desert and Tundra Biome Characteristics

Directions: Complete each box below to describe the characteristics of desert and tundra biomes and the animals that live there.

Desert Biome

1. Draw a picture of your biome.

Characteristics

2. Describe the characteristics of your biome.
   _____
   _____
   _____
   _____
   _____
   _____

Animals

3. List three animals that live in the biome.
   _____
   _____
   _____
   _____
   _____
   _____

Next Page

9.1 Biomes: Desert and Tundra

4. Explain how animals are able to survive in this biome.

Rainforest Biome

5. Draw a picture of your biome.

Characteristics

6. Describe the characteristics of your biome.

Animals

7. List three animals that live in the biome.

8. Explain how animals are able to survive in this biome.

9.2 Biomes: Forests

SCIENCE

Name: _____ Date: _____

Grassland and Aquatic Biomes

Directions: Complete each box below to describe the characteristics of each biome and the animals that live there.

Grassland Biome

1. Draw a picture of your biome.

Characteristics

2. Describe the characteristics of your biome.

Animals

3. List three animals that live in the biome.

9.3 Biomes: Grasslands & Aquatic

Next Page

SCIENCE

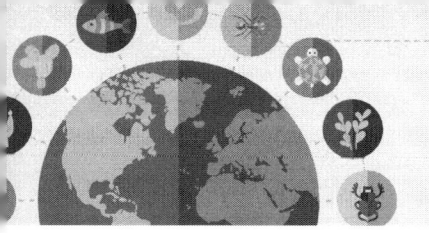

Name: _____   Date: _____

Weather Observations

Directions: In this activity, you will observe the weather. Complete the following activities and answer the questions.

1. Look outside your window or go outside and observe the weather. Follow these steps to fill out the chart.

   a. Record your observations about the weather in the first column.

   b. Next, make a prediction about the weather for the rest of the day. Record your predictions in the middle column.

   c. Then, with the help of your learning coach, look up your local weather forecast for today. Record the forecast in the last column.

Observations	Prediction	Forecast

Next Page

67   11.1 The Weather

2. How did you come up with your prediction for the weather for the remainder of the day?

_____
_____
_____
_____

3. Were your observations and prediction similar to those of the weather forecast? How were they similar or different? Explain.

_____
_____
_____
_____

11.1 The Weather

SCIENCE

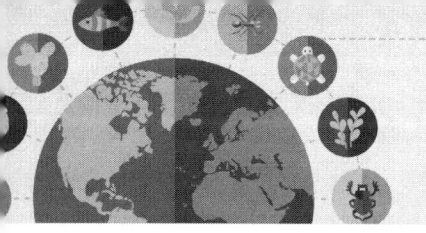

Name: _____ Date: _____

Climate Where You Live

Directions: Think about the climate where you live. Draw a picture of it in each season. Then describe the weather in each of those seasons.

Draw your climate in Spring	Draw your climate in Summer
1. Describe the weather and temperature during this time.	2. Describe the weather and temperature during this time.

Next Page

69 11.3 Climate

Draw your climate in Fall	Draw your climate in Winter

3. Describe the weather and temperature during this time.

_____

_____

_____

_____

4. Describe the weather and temperature during this time.

_____

_____

_____

_____

Think about the weather that you described above. What type of climate do you think you live in?

5. Circle the climate:

Hot   Cold   Temperate

6. Is your climate dry or wet?

_____

_____

11.3 Climate

SCIENCE

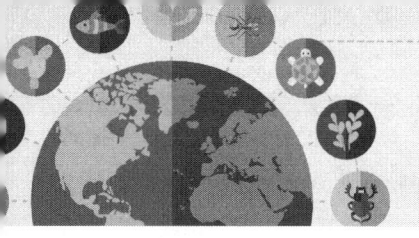

Name: _____ Date: _____

Sun Scientist

Directions: Use what you know about the movement of the Sun and Earth to answer the questions.

1. **Make a Prediction:** You will observe the Sun four times during one day. How do you think the Sun will change throughout that day?
   _____
   _____
   _____
   _____

2. Look out the same window when you wake up in the morning, at lunchtime, at dinnertime, and at bedtime. Draw a picture of where the Sun is located at these times throughout the day. Make sure that you do not look directly at the Sun.

Morning	Lunch

Next Page

71

12.1 Sun Patterns

Dinner	Bedtime

3. Draw a diagram of the Earth revolving around the Sun. Include arrows to explain how the Earth revolves around the Sun and how the Earth rotates as it moves.

4. Write a sentence or two to explain your diagram.

12.1 Sun Patterns

SCIENCE

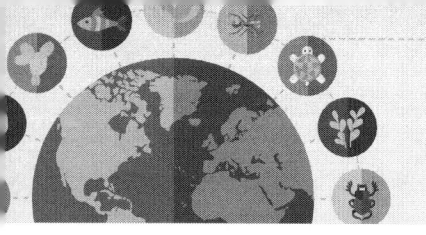

Name: _____   Date: _____

Moon Observation

Directions: Color the phases of the Moon. Make a prediction about what phase the Moon will be in each night. Then draw a picture of what you see.

1. Color the Moon phases.

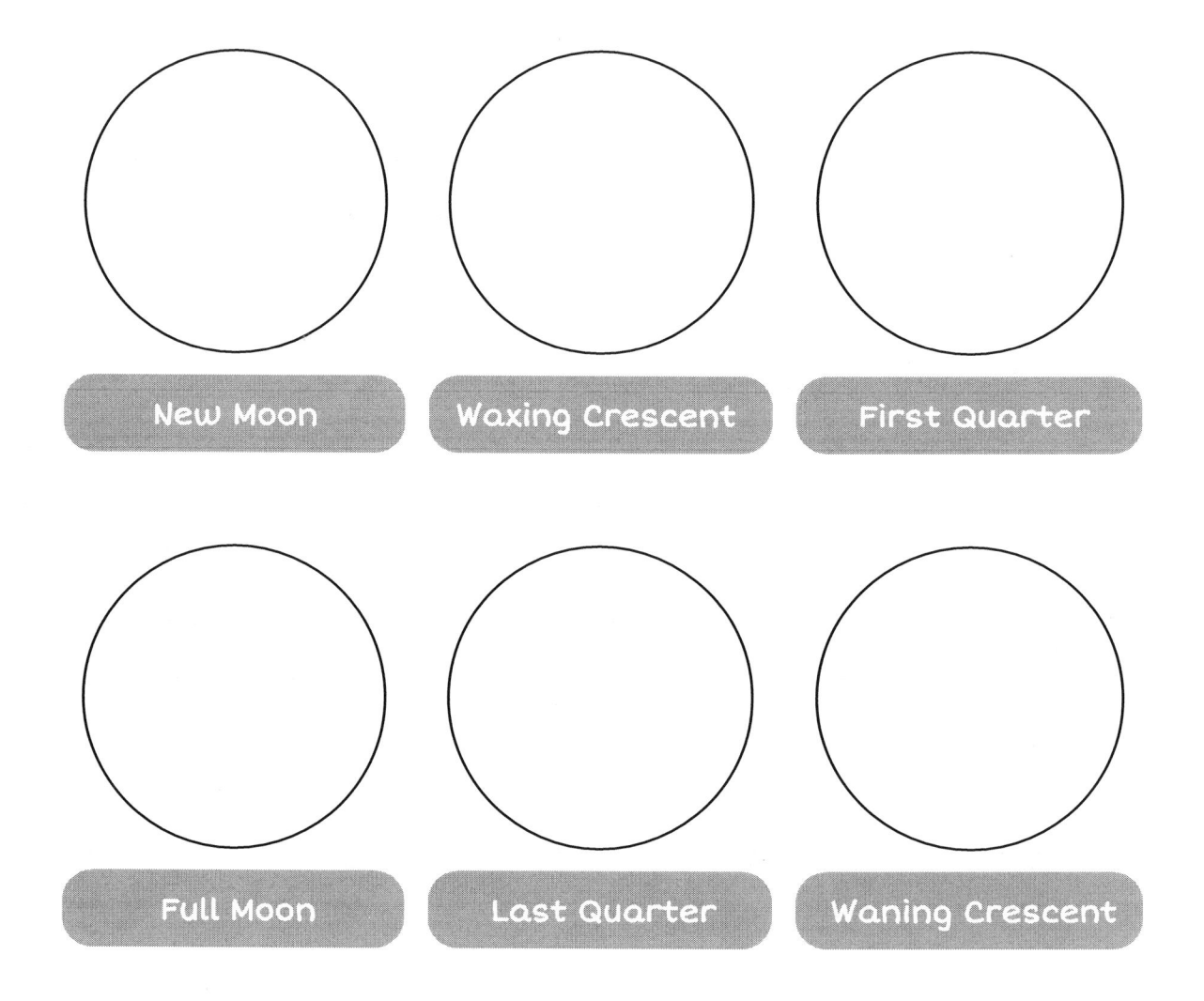

| New Moon | Waxing Crescent | First Quarter |

| Full Moon | Last Quarter | Waning Crescent |

Next Page

73   12.2 Moon Patterns

2. In the first row, draw your prediction of what the Moon will look like each night. Work with your learning coach to find out when the Moon will be visible where you live. Then observe the Moon for four days (or nights). In the second row, draw a picture of what you see.

	Day/Night 1	Day/Night 2	Day/Night 3	Day/Night 4
Prediction of Moon shape				
Actual Moon shape				

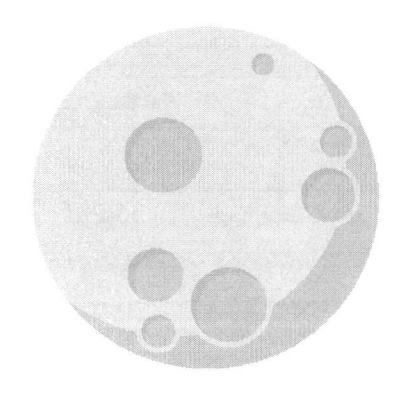

12.2 Moon Patterns

SCIENCE

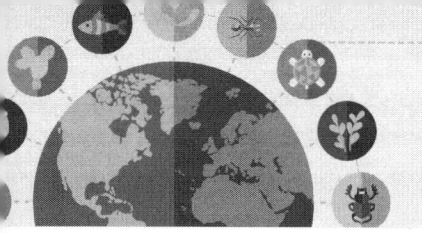

Name: _____ Date: _____

Seasonal Patterns

Directions: Fill in the observation chart. Then answer the following questions.

1. Make predictions about when the Sun will rise and set for four days. Do you notice any patterns? Use your computer or a weather app to find out the exact time of each sunrise and sunset to check your predictions.

	Day 1	Day 2	Day 3	Day 4
Predictions	Sunrise _____ A.M. Sunset _____ P.M.	Sunrise _____ A.M. Sunset _____ P.M.	Sunrise _____ A.M. Sunset _____ P.M.	Sunrise _____ A.M. Sunset _____ P.M.
Actual Time	Sunrise _____ A.M. Sunset _____ P.M.	Sunrise _____ A.M. Sunset _____ P.M.	Sunrise _____ A.M. Sunset _____ P.M.	Sunrise _____ A.M. Sunset _____ P.M.

2. What patterns did you notice from day to day?

_____
_____
_____
_____
_____
_____

Next Page

12.3 Seasonal Patterns

3. Circle the season when the days get shorter.

      Winter   Spring

4. Circle the season when the days get longer.

      Fall   Summer

5. Label each picture with the name of the season that matches the weather.

6. What is your favorite season and why? Answer with a complete sentence.

_____
_____
_____
_____

SCIENCE

Name: _____ Date: _____

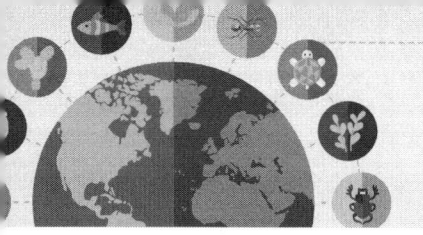

Weather Preparedness

Directions: Research the types of severe weather you receive. Then create a disaster plan and emergency kit.

1. With help from your learning coach, research the types of severe storms or natural disasters that happen where you live. Write them below.

   _____
   _____
   _____
   _____
   _____

2. Draw and label at least five different items that you should include in your weather preparedness kit.

Next Page

3. Explain why you think these items are best for your kit.
_____
_____
_____
_____

4. With help from your learning coach, create a disaster plan for where you live.

Where is a safe place in your home where you can shelter in place?	If you were separated from your family, in what specific places would you meet after the storm?
Room:	Place #1: Place #2:

Where is your emergency kit located?	List up to four emergency contacts (people to contact for help and their phone numbers).
	Name: Phone: Name: Phone: Name: Phone: Name: Phone:

Next Page

12.4 Project: Weather Preparedness

Draw a map of where you live. Then draw an evacuation plan.

5. Explain your evacuation plan in two complete sentences.

_____
_____
_____
_____

Optional: With your learning coach, create a disaster kit in case you encounter any severe storms or natural disasters in the future. Attach a picture of your kit below.

12.4 Project: Weather Preparedness

SCIENCE

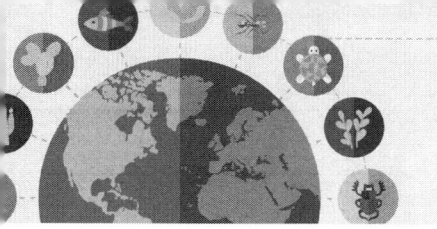

Name: _____ Date: _____

Water Today

Directions: Read the chart below to see the average amount of water each family uses daily. Use this information to help create a chart below to estimate how much water your family uses in one day.

Taking a bath or shower	Flushing the toilet	Washing clothes	Washing hands and brushing teeth
36 Gallons	20 Gallons	15 Gallons	3 Gallons

1. Based on the information above, draw how many gallons of water you think your family uses each day for each activity.

Taking a bath or shower	
Flushing the toilet	
Washing clothes	
Washing hands and brushing teeth	

Next Page

13.1 Fresh Water

80

2. What are some ways that you think you and your family can help cut down on water use?

SCIENCE

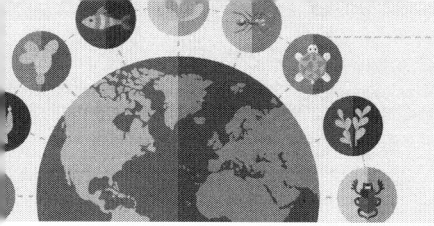

Name: _____ Date: _____

Experiment with Water

Directions: In this activity, you will predict, observe, and record changes in water when heat is added or removed.

> Put a small amount of water in a plastic cup—just enough to cover the bottom of the cup. Follow the instructions in each table.

1.

Instructions	Prediction	Result	Why?
Put your cup in the freezer.	What do you think will happen to the water after 3 hours?	What happened to the water after leaving it in the freezer for 3 hours?	What caused the change to happen?

Next Page

13.2 States of Water

82

2.

Instructions	Prediction	Result	Why?
Take your cup out of the freezer and put it outside or near a window in direct sunlight.	What do you think will happen to the ice after 1 hour?	What happened to the ice after leaving it in the Sun for 1 hour?	What caused the change to happen?

3.

Instructions	Prediction	Result	Why?
Put a pinch or two of salt into the cup. Mix completely. Leave the cup in direct sunlight.	What do you think will happen to the salt and water after 24 hours?	What happened to the salt/water after leaving it for 24 hours?	What caused the change to happen?

Next Page

13.2 States of Water

4. Why do you think the salt was left in your cup, but the water was gone?

SCIENCE

Name: _____ Date: _____

Volume of Water

Directions: Collect 5 different containers from around your home that can hold water and a measuring cup (1 cup). In this activity, you will use containers of different sizes and shapes to compare volume.

1. **Step 1:** Have a grown-up help you use a measuring cup to collect 2 cups of water. This is the volume of water you will use to test each container.

   In each box, draw a picture of each of the 5 containers you will compare today.

Container 1	Container 2	Container 3

Container 4	Container 5

Next Page

85

13.3 Properties of Water

2. **Step 2:** Pour, observe, and compare! Using your measuring cup, pour 2 cups of water into each container. Do not let the water spill! If it gets close to the top, be sure to stop before it overflows.

	Prediction Do you think the container will hold 2 cups of water?	**Results** Did the volume of water fit in the container?
Container 1		
Container 2		
Container 3		
Container 4		
Container 5		

3. Which container held the largest volume of water?
   _____
   _____
   _____

4. Which container held the smallest volume of water?
   _____
   _____
   _____

13.3 Properties of Water

SCIENCE

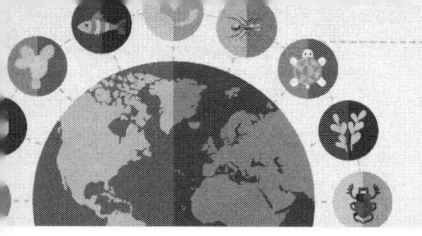

Name: _____   Date: _____

Body of Water Model

Directions: Use what you know about bodies of water to complete the activity and answer the questions.

1. Choose a body of water that is close to where you live. Create a model either by drawing one or building one with materials of your choice. Use the box below to draw your model. If you built your model, take a picture and paste it in the box.

2. Answer the questions below to describe the body of water.

   a. Type of body of water (for example, an ocean, lake, or river):

   _____

   b. Is it a large or small body of water? _____

   c. Is it made of fresh water or salt water? _____

   d. Does it stay still or travel to new places? _____

3. In complete sentences, explain why you think this body of water is located where you live.

_____
_____
_____
_____
_____
_____
_____
_____

14.1 Bodies of Water

SCIENCE

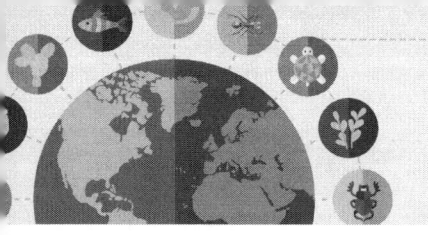

Name: _____ Date: _____

Water Cycle Experiment

Directions: Collect the materials below. Then, follow the steps to complete a quick experiment about the water cycle.

Materials needed
- large bowl
- mug or small cup
- plastic wrap
- string or large rubber band

Step 1: Place the mug or small cup in the center of the bowl. Fill the bowl with water about 2/3 of the way up the outside of the cup. Do not put water inside the cup.

Step 2: Cover the bowl with plastic wrap. Either tie the plastic wrap with a string or place a large rubber band around it to secure it to the bowl.

Step 3: Place the cup and bowl with plastic wrap on it outside in a sunny area for a few hours.

Step 4: After several hours, observe the bowl. The plastic wrap will have condensation on it. Some of the condensation will have dripped or fallen into the cup and the bottom of the bowl.

Step 5: On the next page, draw a picture of what you observed in the box.

Step 6: On your drawing, label the steps in the water cycle: evaporation, condensation, precipitation, collection. Do not forget to include arrows showing which way the cycle goes.

Next Page

14.2 Water Cycle

1. Draw what you observed in the water cycle experiment below. Label the steps of the water cycle in your drawing.

2. Explain what happened in the experiment and why you think this happened.

14.2 Water Cycle

SCIENCE

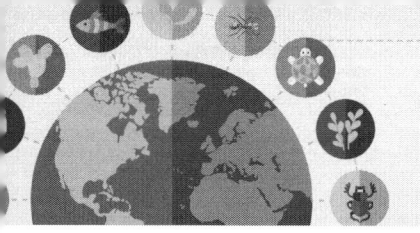

Name: _____ Date: _____

Watershed Experiment

Directions: Gather the materials below. Follow the directions to make a model of a watershed. Then answer the questions.

Materials:
- piece of cardboard
- paper
- tape
- green and blue markers
- spray bottle with water

Directions:

Step 1: Crumple a piece of paper gently, not into a tight ball.

Step 2: Unfold the piece of paper, but do not flatten it. Tape the corners of the paper to the cardboard.

Step 3: With the green marker, color the tops of the fold right along the wrinkles. The green marker represents land.

Step 4: With the blue marker, color the bottoms of the folds, where the rivers and lakes would be. The blue represents the bottom of the watershed, where the water collects after traveling over the ground.

Step 5: Use the spray bottle to spray water on top of the piece of paper. Watch how the water moves the colors of the markers.

Next Page

14.3 Watersheds

1. Paste or draw a picture of your model watershed in the box below.

2. In complete sentences, explain what you think is happening in this experiment.

3. In complete sentences, explain what you can do to help keep watersheds clean.

14.3 Watersheds

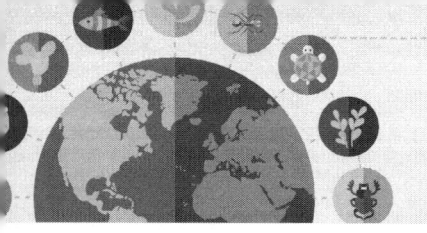

Name: _____   Date: _____

Animal Extinction

Directions: Read each scenario below. Write a sentence about what you think will happen next. Draw a picture to illustrate your sentence. Then answer the question below.

Scenario	Description	Picture
1. A bird species lives on an island without humans. Then, a group of people arrive on the island and hunt the birds for food. The people brought animals to the island. The animals eat the birds and their eggs too. Over time, there were fewer and fewer birds. What do you think happened to the birds?		
2. Trees in a forest are being cleared. This is destroying the shelter and food sources of the flying squirrel. What could happen to this species?		

Next Page

93   15.1 Extinct Animals

3. What is something that can cause animals to go extinct?

_____

_____

_____

_____

_____

_____

15.1 Extinct Animals

SCIENCE

Name: _____   Date: _____

Sea Turtles

Directions: Color the picture below. Then answer the question.

Next Page

95   15.2 Endangered Animals

1. Sea turtles are endangered because they eat plastic in the ocean water. What can you do to help the population of sea turtles grow?

15.2 Endangered Animals

SCIENCE

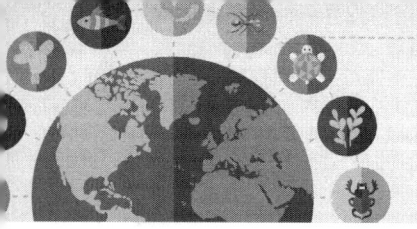

Name: _____ Date: _____

Dinosaurs vs. Birds

Directions: Think about what you have learned about dinosaurs and birds. Do you believe that dinosaurs are birds?

1. Give at least two reasons to support your answer. Be sure to use evidence and examples.

_____
_____
_____
_____
_____

2. Draw a picture to support your opinion in the box below.

97

15.4 Project: Dinosaurs vs. Birds

SCIENCE

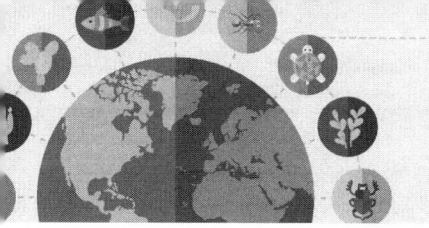

Name: _____ Date: _____

Identify the Animals by Traits

Directions: Look at each group of animals. Follow the directions within each box.

1. Circle the animals that have feathers.

2. Circle the animals that hide in shells.

3. Circle the animals that have fur.

4. Circle the animals that move only by swimming.

5. Circle the animals that move fast.

6. Circle the animals that move slowly.

Next Page

16.1 Animal Characteristics

98

7. Circle the animals that are aggressive.	8. Circle the animals that are gentle.	9. Circle the animals that live only in water.

16.1 Animal Characteristics

SCIENCE

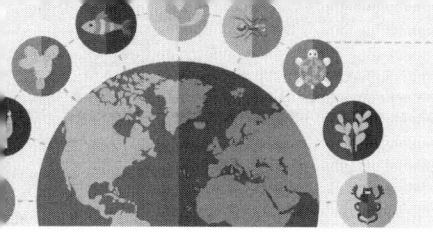

Name: _____   Date: _____

Warm-Blooded and Cold-Blooded Animal Search

Directions: Look at each group of animals. Follow the directions within each box.

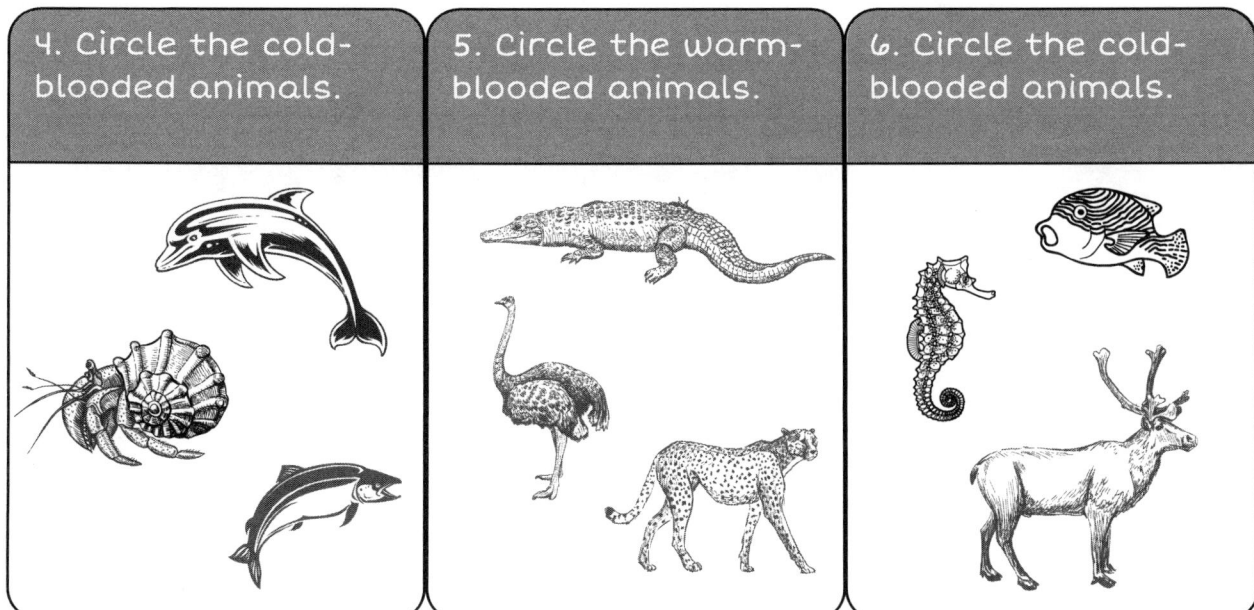

1. Circle the warm-blooded animals.	2. Circle the cold-blooded animals.	3. Circle the warm-blooded animals.
4. Circle the cold-blooded animals.	5. Circle the warm-blooded animals.	6. Circle the cold-blooded animals.

16.3 Warm and Cold-Blooded Animals

100

SCIENCE

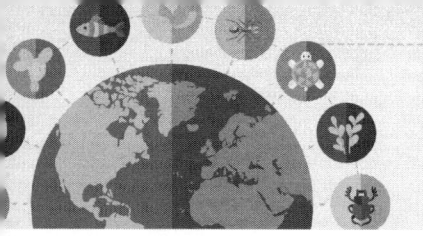

Name: _____   Date: _____

Bird-Watching

Directions: Take some time to observe birds in your area. Use the steps below to help you with your observations.

Step 1: Find a place outside or near a window to observe bird activity.

Step 2: Ask yourself the following questions: Where do the birds live? How do they find food? How do they communicate? How does the weather or season affect them?

Step 3: What do the birds look like? How can you use your sense of sight to describe their color, size, and the activities you observe?

Step 4: Observe their songs. Can you tell the difference between the different sounds and songs of different birds? Why do you think they are making the sounds?

In the box below, draw some of the different birds you observed. Then answer the questions below.

17.1 Characteristics of Birds

1. Where do the birds live?

2. Where do the birds eat?

3. How did the birds communicate?

4. If you saw any nests, where were they located?

17.1 Characteristics of Birds

SCIENCE

Name: _____ Date: _____

Build a Nest

Directions: Follow the steps below to weave your very own bird's nest, just as the weaver finch did in the video. Use materials from inside or outside your home to help build a strong nest. When you are finished, take a picture of your nest, and submit it to your teacher.

Steps

1. Search inside and outside your home and collect materials to build your nest. You can use twigs, moss, feathers, grass, string, twine, etc. Do not use tape or glue.
2. Use the weaving technique from the video to create the nest by weaving the materials in and out to hold them together.
3. Test the strength of your nest by adding rocks to represent eggs.
4. Answer the questions below.
5. Take a picture of your nest and submit it to your teacher with this worksheet.

1. What materials did you use to build your nest?
   _____
   _____
   _____
   _____
   _____

Next Page

17.2 Different Nests for Different Birds

2. How were you able to make your nest strong and not fall apart?

3. How many rocks was your nest able to hold?

4. What type of nest did you build?

5. Where do you think a bird would build this nest?

17.2 Different Nests for Different Birds

SCIENCE

Name: _____   Date: _____

Unique Nests

Directions: Draw a picture of a weaverbird nest and a swiftlet nest in the spaces provided. Then answer the questions below.

1. Draw the Weaverbird and Swiflet nests in the correct box.

Weaverbird Nest	Swiftlet Nest

2. What makes these nests unique?

_____
_____
_____
_____

Next Page

105   17.3 Unique Birds

3. Draw a line to the word on the right that correctly completes each sentence.

a. Male weaverbirds hang upside down from their _____ when they are finished to try to attract a mate.

b. Swiftlets are in _____ because humans are harvesting their nests.

c. Both swiftlets and weaverbirds are very _____. They live in large groups, or communities.

d. Swiftlets use _____, or clicking sounds, to find their nests in dark caves.

e. Weaverbirds build nests that hang from tree branches to make it harder for _____ to get to them.

echolocation

predators

nests

social

danger

17.3 Unique Birds

SCIENCE

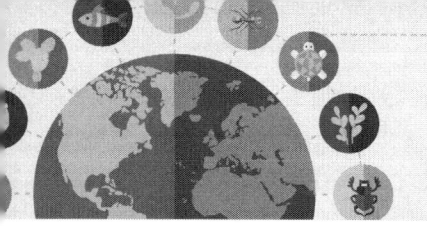

Name: _____ Date: _____

Match the Reptile

Directions: Draw a line to match each reptile with its correct habitat. There may be more than one reptile that can live in each habitat.

1. What do all of the habitats of reptiles have in common?

_____
_____
_____
_____

107   18.1 Characteristics of Reptiles

SCIENCE

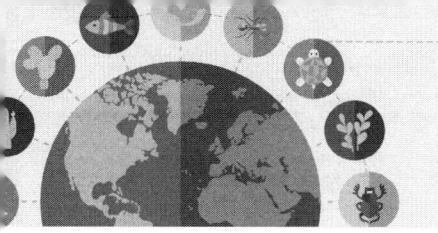

Name: _____ Date: _____

Fish Features

Directions: Use what you know of fish to complete the following activities.

1. In the first column of the table below, write the correct fish feature from the word bank. Then draw a fish and label each feature.

   gills   fins   scales   backbone

Feature	Purpose
	This feature helps support all the other bones in the body of a fish.
	These protect a fish's body and help it move smoothly through the water.
	These help fish swim.
	These help fish breathe underwater.

2. Draw a fish in its correct habitat below and label its features: backbone, scales, fins, and gills.

18.3 Characteristics of Fish

SCIENCE

Name: _____   Date: _____

Cold-Blooded Habitat

Directions: This pond habitat is home to different cold-blooded animals. Draw one amphibian, one reptile, and one fish in the habitat. Then complete the chart below.

1. Draw one amphibian, one reptile, and one fish in this habitat. Make sure to put the animal where they would most likely be or live.

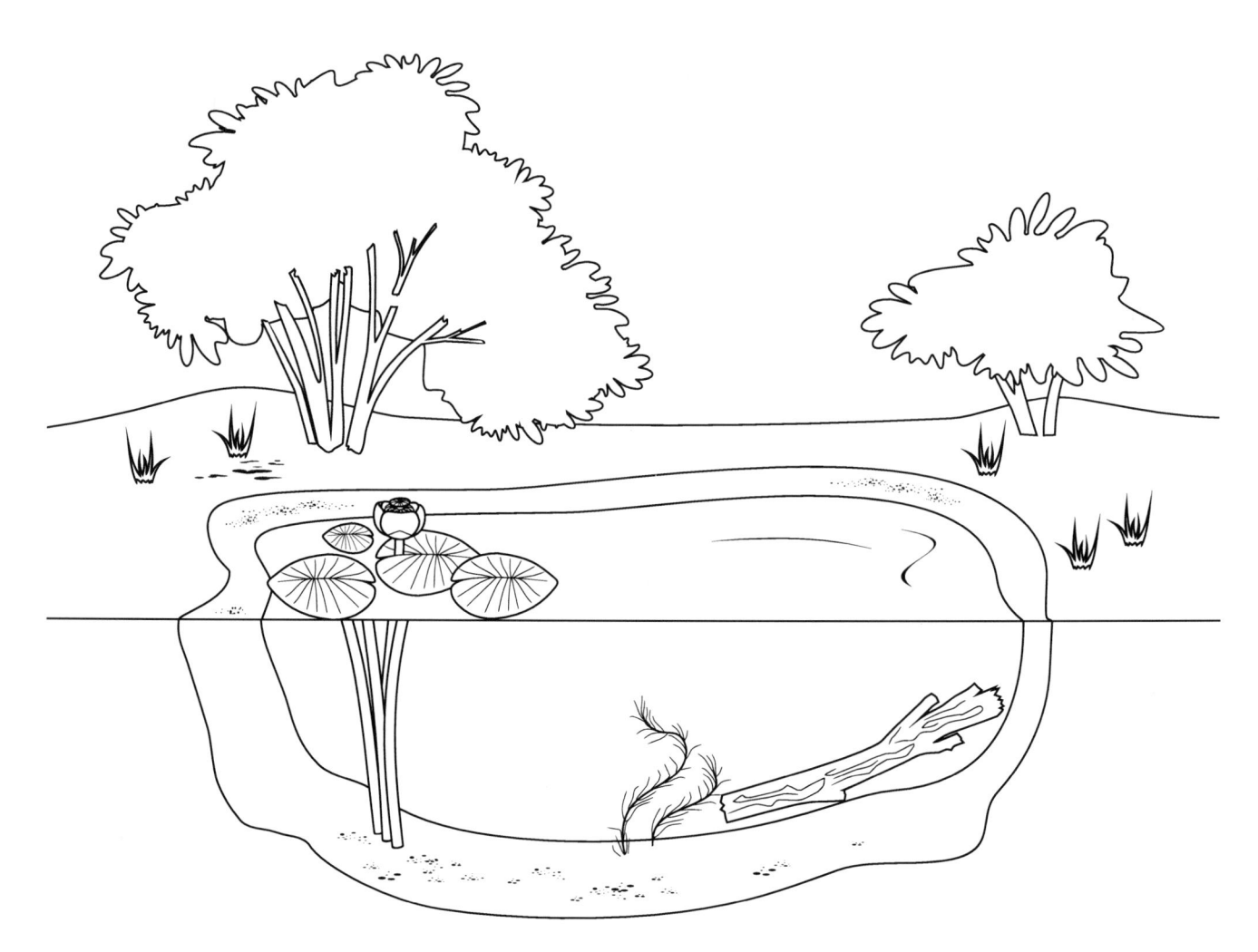

Next Page

109   18.4 Project: Cold-Blooded Habitat

2. Fill in this chart with the information that matches your three animals.

Cold-Blooded Animal Group	Animal Name (animal drawn in the habitat)	Habitat (where in or around the pond the animal lives)	Characteristics (characteristics of the animal)
Reptile			
Amphibian			
Fish			

3. How are these animals similar?

4. How are these animals different?

18.4 Project: Cold-Blooded Habitat

Cutout Worksheets

SCIENCE

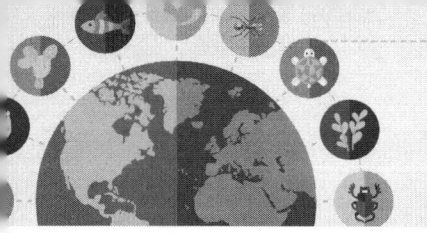

Name: _____ Date: _____

Animal Tracks Sorting

Directions: Cut out each set of animal tracks along the dotted lines. Then glue the tracks in the correct category.

Diagonal Walkers

Gallopers

Bounders

Pacers

Next Page

113   3.1 Tracks Animals Make

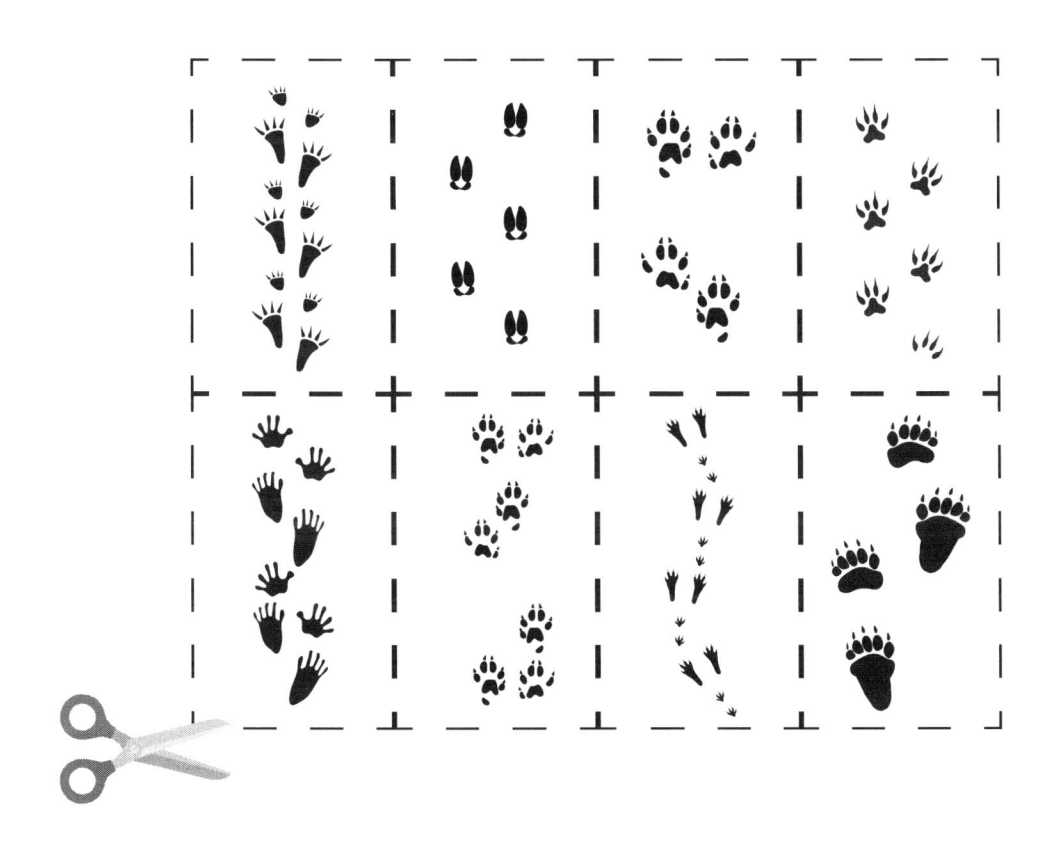

3.1 Tracks Animals Make

SCIENCE

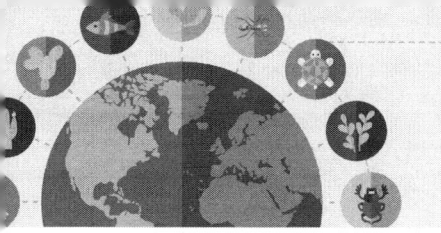

Name: _____ Date: _____

Living and Nonliving Ocean Sort

Directions: Look at the images and descriptions below. Decide if each one is living or nonliving and write the name in the correct column. Then answer the questions.

1. Cut out each item at the end of the worksheet and paste it into the living or the nonliving column.

Living	Nonliving

10.1 Salt Water

Next Page

116

2. What things did you place in the living column? Why?

_____
_____
_____
_____
_____

3. What things did you place in the nonliving column? Why?

_____
_____
_____
_____
_____

10.1 Salt Water

118

SCIENCE

Name: _____ Date: _____

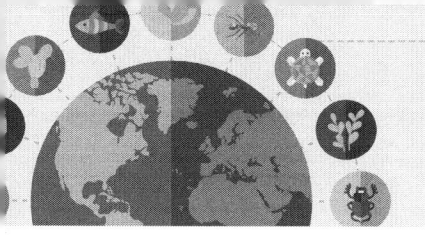

Design an Aquatic Habitat

Directions: Cut out the images along the dotted lines. Decide which items are needed in an aquatic habitat. Then glue them on the aquarium picture to design an aquatic habitat.

1. Why did you include these things in your aquatic habitat?

_____
_____
_____
_____
_____

Next Page

10.3 Aquatic Habitats

122

SCIENCE

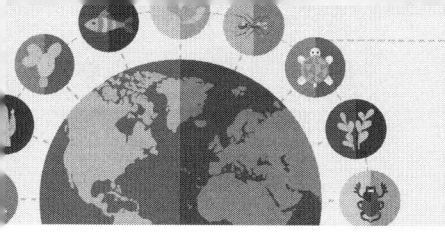

Name: _____ Date: _____

What to Do?

Directions: It is important to pay attention to the weather forecast when you are making plans. Look at the weather forecast for each day. Cut out the cards along the dotted lines. Decide which clothes and activities would be best for each type of weather. Paste each card in the correct weather column. Then answer the question below.

90° F	50° F	25° F

Next Page

11.2 Weather and You

124

1. How would your sunny-day activities change if the temperature was only 60 degrees?

11.2 Weather and You

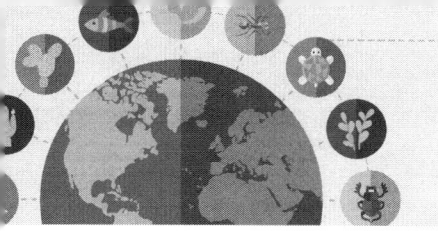

Name: _____   Date: _____

Making Migrations

Directions: Cut out the cards on the next page along the dotted lines. Read each scenario, and sort each card into the correct column: Migration or Hibernation.

Migration	Hibernation

Next Page

15.3 Animal Adaptations

1. Look at the pictures of the arctic fox below. Why do you think it has two different types of fur?

_____
_____
_____
_____
_____
_____

Animals move to another place to find shelter, food, and water.	The gopher digs its burrow underground so it can sleep until it can easily find food in the spring.	Animals go into a deep sleep during the winter.
Lizards find an unused burrow to settle in during the winter because they cannot survive cold temperatures.	Gray whales spend the summer feeding in the waters near Alaska. In the fall, they move back to warm waters near Mexico to have their babies.	Monarch butterflies move to warmer climates during the winter and return in the spring to lay eggs.
Bears eat a lot in the weeks leading up to winter before the cold weather makes it hard to find food. Then they go to sleep until spring.	Geese fly in a V pattern to warmer climates during the cold months so they can find food to eat.	

15.3 Animal Adaptations

130

SCIENCE

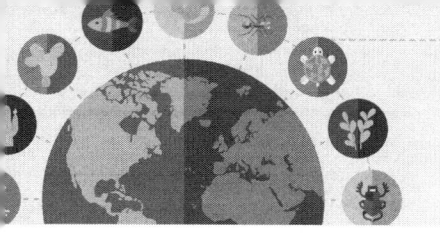

Name: _____   Date: _____

Vertebrate and Invertebrate Sort

Directions: Cut out the pictures of animals. Decide if they are vertebrates or invertebrates. Then glue them in the correct column in the chart. Answer the question below.

1. Animal Sort

Vertebrates	Invertebrates

Next Page

16.2 Vertebrates and Invertebrates

132

2. Why did you place the animals where you did? What could you tell about the animals that made you choose vertebrate or invertebrate?

16.2 Vertebrates and Invertebrates

SCIENCE

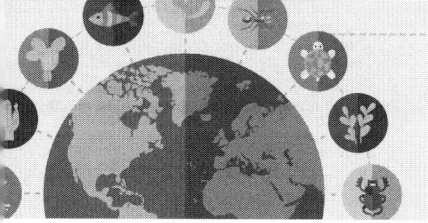

Name: _____ Date: _____

Amphibian Habitats

Directions: Cut out each habitat image below along the dotted lines. Then sort the habitats into the correct columns. If the habitat is suitable for an amphibian, paste it in the Amphibian Habitat column. If it is not suitable for an amphibian, paste it in the Not for Amphibians column.

Amphibian Habitat	Not for Amphibians

1. What habitats do amphibians need to survive?

   _____
   _____
   _____
   _____
   _____
   _____

Next Page

18.2 Characteristics of Amphibians

18.2 Characteristics of Amphibians

138

ACCELERATE EDUCATION

© 2023 by Accelerate Education
Visit us on the Web at: www.accelerate.education
ISBN: 978-1-63916-114-0